# CREEPY KILLER PLANTS

LIFE ON THE EDGE

T0009919

## BIOLOGY AT ITS MOST EXTREME!

CHERITON
CHILDREN'S BOOKS

Published in 2023 by **Cheriton Children's Books**
1 Bank Drive West, Shrewsbury, Shropshire, SY3 9DJ, UK

© 2023 Cheriton Children's Books

First Edition

Authors: Kelly Roberts and Louise Spilsbury
Designer: Paul Myerscough
Editor: Louisa Simmons
Proofreader: Jessica Edwards

Picture credits: Cover: Shutterstock/Kuttelvaserova Stuchelova; Inside: p1: Shutterstock/
JTKP; p4: Shutterstock/Ernie Cooper; p5: Shutterstock/dpd0302; p6: Shutterstock/
Kuttelvaserova Stuchelova; p7: Shutterstock/Linas T; p8: Shutterstock/D. Kucharski
K. Kucharska; p9: Shutterstock/Luka Hercigonja; p10: Shutterstock/ZayacSK; p11:
Shutterstock/JTKP; p12: Shutterstock/Daleen Loest; p13: Shutterstock/JRJfin; p14:
Shutterstock/Simon Groewe; p15: Shutterstock/Sue J Hill Photography; p16: Shutterstock/
Don Landwehrle; p17: Shutterstock/Karel Bock; p18: Shutterstock/Dmitry Naumov; p19:
Shutterstock/Ro_ksy; p20: Shutterstock/Orest Lyzhechka; p21: Shutterstock/Evgeiia;
p22: Shutterstock/Yusuf Madi; p23: Shutterstock/Piotr Milewski; p24: Shutterstock/
Fritz16; p25: Shutterstock/Attraction Art; p26: Shutterstock/ArgenLant; p27: Shutterstock/
Chrispo; p28: Shutterstock/Cpaulfell; p29: Shutterstock/Hordynski Photography; p30:
Shutterstock/Paulo Nishizawa; p31: Shutterstock/Christian Vinces; p32: Shutterstock/
Mivod; p33: Shutterstock/O Partime Photo; p34: Shutterstock/ImageBroker.com; p35:
Shutterstock/Christian Forster; p36: Shutterstock/Bernd Schmidt; p37: Shutterstock/
Tommy Lee Walker; p38: Shutterstock/HVPMdev; p39: Shutterstock/Adrian_am13;
p40: Shutterstock/Wasanajai; p41: Shutterstock/Irina Kononova; p42: Shutterstock/
Fivepointsix; p43: Shutterstock/Riki Irawanda; p44: Shutterstock/Plasid; p45:
Shutterstock/Amalia Gruber.

Printed in China

Please visit our website,
www.cheritonchildrensbooks.com
to see more of our high-quality books.

## WHAT'S ON THE COVER?

A fly is doomed—
trapped in the leaves
of a Venus flytrap.

Page 1: a pitcher
plant (see page 11).

# CONTENTS

# CHAPTER 1

# PLANTS THAT EAT MEAT

When we think of plants, we imagine docile **organisms**, and most of the plants in the world are just that. However, there are some that are far from docile! These plants have extreme features or behaviors that help them survive, **reproduce**, or get food. **Carnivorous**, or flesh-eating, plants are one of those organisms. Most plants make their own food from sunlight and air using a process called **photosynthesis** —but carnivorous plants get some of the **nutrients** they need to live by eating **insects** and other small animals.

## Sunny By Name, Not Sunny By Nature!

The sundew has a soft and gentle ring to its name, but the plant is anything but gentle! It lives in wet and often sandy places, where the plant cannot find all the nutrients it needs in the soil. To get around this problem, the sundew has a smart and deadly plan. It catches and eats small animals, such as insects.

*Insects are trapped by the sticky substance on the sundew's leaves.*

## Stuck and Eaten

In Australia, there is a sundew plant that has some extra-long hairs. They stretch out like tentacles around the edge of the leaf, and when these hairs sense an insect, they flip or catapult the creature into the center of the leaf. There, it is trapped on the sticky hairs and **digested**.

*The sticky hairs on the sundew's leaves glisten like dew in the sunshine.*

# BRUTAL BIOLOGY

Sundews have hairs covering their leaves, which work a little like sticky flypaper. Once an insect is stuck to the hairs, it cannot escape. The hairs slowly curl up and wrap themselves around their **prey**. Eventually, the whole leaf wraps around the prey. Then, the insect victim is slowly digested and absorbed by the plant.

## Monstrous Meat Eater

The Venus flytrap is a deadly plant that is monstrous in the way it finds its food. In fact, the killer plant would not be out of place in a horror movie. Thankfully, the Venus flytrap does not eat people! But it does have a pretty terrifying way of catching flies and other prey.

## A Spiky End

The leaves of the Venus flytrap form an amazing trap. At the end of each leaf there is a folding part that can open and close like jaws. Around 14 to 20 spikes stick out from the edges of this trap. On the surface inside the leaves are tiny hairs that work like triggers—if an insect lands on a leaf and touches two of these hairs within a short space of time, the leaf closes. The spikes form a cage from which the insect caught inside cannot escape.

*The leaves of this Venus flytrap have shut tightly around a fly.*

In just a few seconds, the leaves of this Venus flytrap will snap shut, and the fly will be trapped.

## Eaten Slowly

Once the insect is caught, the trap closes tighter and tighter to squash the prey. The plant also makes a sticky substance to seal the gaps around the edge of the trap, where the two sides meet. Then special substances called **enzymes** are released. They break down the prey's body into pieces small enough for the plant to absorb.

## BRUTAL BIOLOGY

Once an insect has been digested, the Venus flytrap opens its leaves again, and the plant waits for another meal to come along. The plant is not a fussy eater—even small frogs are trapped in its fast-moving, toothed leaves!

## Floating Killer

Lurking in the water, a floating killer lies in wait for its prey—the bladderwort. This hungry meat-eater lives in lakes, bogs, and streams, waiting for prey to pass. The bladderwort plant gets its name from tiny pouches called bladders that grow from its **stem**. The plant sucks small prey into the bladders and then eats them.

*The pouches of the bladderwort can be seen under a microscope.*

## Sucked Inside

Bladders on a bladderwort are hollow chambers with a flexible door. The plant gets the bladders ready for action by emptying the water out of them. This makes the pressure inside the bladders much lower than the surrounding water, which creates sucking power.

## Death Trap

The plant has tiny hairs at the opening of the bladder, which work like triggers. When a small animal passes by, it creates currents in the water. They make the hairs move. Then, the bladder door suddenly opens, the passing prey is sucked in, and the door quickly closes again. The door seals around the prey, and it is slowly digested.

# BRUTAL BIOLOGY

Bladderworts can move incredibly quickly, in fact, the door of a bladder can open and close in about a millisecond. There are 1,000 milliseconds in a second! The plant moves so fast that it is impossible for the human eye to see.

*Bladderworts float because they have hollow stems. They may look pretty, but they are deadly.*

## Lurking Killer

Within the **tropical** rain forest lurks a deadly killer—the pitcher plant. This cunning carnivore eats insects that fall inside its deadly trap. The plant has hollow structures at the tips of its leaves, which are shaped like pitchers with open lids. Any insect that falls inside becomes a quick and tasty meal for the sneaky killer plant!

*The pitcher has a lid to stop rain filling it up.*

## A Sweet Death

The killer plant first attracts visiting insects with the bright purple and pink colors of its pitchers, but it is the smell of sweet **nectar** inside the **glands** under the pitcher lid that really draws in prey. Some pitcher plants even add chemicals to their nectar, which slow insects down, so they are more likely to fall into the lethal traps.

## No Escape

Pitcher plants make sure their victims can never escape. The lip of the pitcher leaf is covered with downward-pointing hairs that stop insects from climbing out of the top when they fall into the trap. Below the lip, are smooth, hairless, and waxy walls. If an insect does try to climb out, they simply slide back down. The prey falls into a pool of liquid at the bottom of the pitcher, and drowns. Then, enzymes turn the insect into a mushy liquid meal.

## BRUTAL BIOLOGY

The largest pitcher plant in the world doesn't need to trap prey, because it is a poop-eater! Small mammals called tree shrews perch on the lip of the 12-inch- (30 cm) wide pitcher, and feed on the nectar inside. As they do so, they poop into the pitcher, and the plant feeds on the poop!

# CHAPTER 2

# TOTALLY TOXIC

Many plants are poisonous, to defend themselves. The plants use the poison to stop animals eating or touching them. The poison can make animals very sick—even if they just touch the plants—and some can even kill them. People are sometimes made very sick or even killed by touching poisonous plants, too.

## Like a Doll

The doll's eyes plant is an unusual wildflower that grows up to 3 feet (90 cm) high, and has a distinctive **fruit**. The plant is called "doll's eyes" because it has shiny white berries with red spots, which look a little like the eyes of a china doll. The berries grow at the top of the plant's thick, blood-red stems.

*Fortunately, the fruit of the doll's eyes tastes so bad that most people never try more than one berry.*

*The berries of the doll's eyes look uncannily like eyes!*

## Killer Eyes

There is nothing doll-like about the berries of the doll's eyes—they contain deadly **toxins**. In fact, most animals know to leave the plant alone to avoid certain death. The berries from the doll's eyes plant are so poisonous that eating just five or six can make a person or animal extremely sick, and eating more could kill them.

# BRUTAL BIOLOGY

Birds have a great defense against doll's eyes berries—they are **immune** to the toxins and can eat them without being harmed. The toxins do not harm the birds because the plant wants birds to eat its berries, so it can then spread the seeds inside. When the birds poop out the seeds that were inside the fruits, they grow somewhere new.

## Nasty Nightshade

The name "deadly nightshade" has a lethal ring to it, and rightly so. This plant is very dangerous. It grows in the shade of trees in woods or on wastelands, and its shiny black berries are highly poisonous.

## Poison Peril

The deadly nightshade plant can grow as high as 6 feet (2 m) tall. It has deep-purple or deep-blue flowers with orange or yellow **stamens**, with stalks in the middle of the flowers. The stem, leaves, berries, and **roots** of this plant contain poisons called atropine and scopolamine. But it is the berries that are most poisonous, and they taste incredible sweet. In fact, they are so sweet that animals cannot resist eating them, and when they do, the poison **paralyzes** their muscles and kills them.

*Some birds can eat the berries of the deadly nightshade without being harmed by them.*

*The deadly nightshade has beautiful flowers around its lethal berries.*

## On the Menu

Sometimes, people cook and eat plants that are closely related to the deadly nightshade. People eat tomatoes, chili peppers, and cooked potatoes or eggplants, which are all relatives of the nightshade. But people should never eat the leaves from those plants because they contain toxins that can be harmful.

## BRUTAL BIOLOGY

The **species** name for deadly nightshade contains the word "belladonna," which means beautiful woman in Italian. There is a legend that long ago some women in Italy were foolish enough to eat deadly nightshade because it made the pupils of their eyes widen, which they thought made them look more beautiful. This was highly dangerous, and no one would ever do that today. However, people have used extracts of the atropine poisons in deadly nightshade to make a medicine that helps doctors widen patients' pupils to prepare for eye surgery.

## Deadly as a Snake

The snakeroot is a native plant of North America. It was named "snakeroot" because early settlers in the United States believed that its roots could cure people who had been bitten by snakes. But the plant did not help people, rather, it poisoned them!

## Killing Settlers

When settlers first arrived in the United States, they did not know about the dangers of snakeroot, and many thousands were killed by the plant. The illness brought on by contact with the plant's poisons became known as milk sickness. President Abraham Lincoln's mother is believed to have died from milk sickness in 1818, when she was just 34 years old.

*Farm animals are most often poisoned by snakeroot.*

## Animal Killer

Snakeroot flower heads are several inches across and contain many white flowers. The flowers produce black seeds with small tufts of white hair. They work a little like parachutes, to carry seeds on the wind so snakeroot plants spread far away. The snakeroot plant contains a lethal toxin known as tremetol, to keep animals from eating it. When livestock such as cattle, horses, goats, and sheep eat large quantities of the plant, it can kill them.

*Snakeroot plants can spread quickly.*

# BRUTAL BIOLOGY

When cattle and sheep eat snakeroot, their meat and milk become poisonous, too. That is because they are contaminated with the plant's toxins. Calves and lambs may die from drinking their mothers' milk. If humans drink milk or eat beef from contaminated cattle they can become sick with milk sickness.

## Pet Killer

Lilies are popular plants that many people like to have in their backyards. People also buy lilies to give as gifts or to have in their own homes. But, pretty as they are, these plants can be deadly. In fact, they kill pets every year after people bring the plants into their homes.

## A Killer in Disguise

People often buy lilies because these flowers look unusual. They also have a very strong scent, which many people love to smell. But several types of lily, such as Easter lily, tiger lily, and rubrum lily, add more than just a scent to a room. They carry poison that is a pet killer. If a cat eats even a small amount of a lily, it can kill it, because the toxin damages the animal's kidneys. Any animal that comes into contact with the dangerous plant must immediately be taken to the vet.

*The stunning Easter lily, with its trumpet-shaped, white flowers, is a native of Japan.*

## Poison Everywhere

Every part of the lily plant is poisonous. That includes its leaf, stem, and flower. However, the **pollen** contains the most toxins. Pollen is a fine powder found on the stamens that stand up like tiny stalks in the center of a flower.

*Some lilies come with a health warning that they are dangerous to pets such as cats.*

## BRUTAL BIOLOGY

Cats can be affected by pollen if some falls on their fur or if they brush up against lily flowers. When a cat licks and grooms its fur later, it may swallow the poisonous powder.

# CHAPTER 3

# KILLERS WITHIN

Insects have many different life cycles. Some last a few days, Parasites are living things that exist on or in other living things, which are known as **hosts**. Not only do parasites live in or on other organisms, they also steal from them, by taking their food. By doing so, parasites can weaken or harm the host. However, they do not hurt it enough to kill it—they need their host to stay alive in order to feed on it.

*Dodder grows into and grasps onto other plants.*

## Takeaway Meals

Most parasitic plants tap into their host's stems. There, water that contains nutrients can be found. By tapping into a host's water supply, the parasite does not need to grow its own roots to take up water and nutrients from soil. Some parasitic plants can also make their own food by creating sugars. This process is called photosynthesis. The parasites carry out photosynthesis in their hosts' leaves.

## Eaten Alive

Dodder is a plant that looks a little like the strands of string or spaghetti. It does not have leaves, so cannot make its own food through photosynthesis. Instead, it grows upward and outward, and twines around other plants. It then pushes out special parts, called haustoria, from its stem. They burrow into the plants the dodder has wrapped itself around, and feed on the nutrients inside them.

*This dodder has wrapped itself around a potato plant. Dodder is dangerous to crops because it can take over entire crop fields.*

# BRUTAL BIOLOGY

Some types of dodder plants produce more than 16,000 seeds. Once they land in soil, the seeds can survive there for up to 60 years, waiting for rain. Once the soil is moist and the sun is shining, each seed sprouts roots and a thin yellow stem that grows upward. The stem then feels its way through the air, until it makes contact with a host to feed on.

## Super Stinker

The biggest flower in the world is a parasite known as *rafflesia arnoldii*, or the corpse flower. Each single red-and-white spotted flower on the plant measures 3 feet (1 m) across. The worst thing about the giant is that it has a terrible stench—it smells like rotting flesh! It grows in the rain forests of Borneo, in Southeast Asia.

## Plant Invasion

The corpse flower spends most of its life out of sight, living inside the stem or roots of woody vines that run under the forest floor. The plant can only be seen when its flower buds start to grow from the ground. As they do so, they resemble dark mushrooms, but they soon open, swell, and grow. They are huge, red, and fleshy—and like no other plant on Earth.

*The rafflesia is huge —and very stinky!*

When a corpse flower stops blooming, its color fades and darkens.

## Insect Magnet

At the heart of each corpse flower bloom is a column, which carries a disk with male or female parts. As the flower warms, it makes a horrible stink. Flies climb inside, attracted by the smell, which they think is rotting flesh. As they crawl inside, they rub pollen from male parts onto female parts and the rafflesia starts to make seeds.

## BRUTAL BIOLOGY

The corpse flower creates heat to make the chemicals that smell so badly. It does so by making a lot of carbon dioxide gas. The gas makes visiting insects drowsy, so they spend more time on the stinky flowers and help **pollinate** the plant.

*The Australian Christmas tree can grow beautiful flowers only because it feeds on other plants.*

## Not Very Festive

The giant of the parasitic plant world is the Australian Christmas tree—it stands 30 feet (9 m) tall. When young, this plant makes its own food by photosynthesis and drawing up nutrients from the soil. But when it becomes an adult, the plant looks to nearby plants for its meals.

## Christmas Killer

In western Australia, the dry season happens around Christmas. Despite this, one plant flowers as if it is constantly raining. This is the Australian Christmas tree. It thrives when other plants struggle by killing its nearby fellow plants. It taps into their roots and steals their water and nutrients. This killer feeds on many types of plants, from grasses to shrubs, finding a meal wherever it can.

## Seek and Take

The Australian Christmas tree's long roots grow and spread underground, until they reach a host. Then, the tip of the killer's root forms a white ring around the host root. Inside the ring is a sharp, scissor-shaped part that slices into the host's root. It then connects with the tubes inside, which carry water and nutrients. Next, the parasite redirects the nutrient-rich flow of water into its own roots.

# BRUTAL BIOLOGY

The Australian Christmas tree is related to the mistletoe plant, which grows on trees such as oak. Birds feed on mistletoe berries, and as they do so, the sticky seeds inside the berries stick to their beaks. When the birds fly to another tree, they wipe their beaks on a branch, and the mistletoe seeds may then begin to grow there.

*The mistletoe tree has beautiful white berries.*

# CHAPTER 4

# ARMED AND DANGEROUS

Plants have many different ways of stopping large animals from damaging or eating them. Some stab and sting! These aggressive plants have jagged thorns or sharp spikes that put off animals that might try and eat them, or they have a scary substance that can sting.

## Hairy Hurter

The leaves and stems of a stinging nettle are covered with tiny hairs that deliver a painful sting. While this defense may keep away grazing animals, insects are not affected by the hairs. They simply land on the plants, feed on them, and then carry their pollen to other stinging nettles. The insects are unharmed by the hairs because the plant needs the tiny creatures to carry its pollen.

*A sting from a stinging nettle can be very painful.*

*The hairs on a stinging nettle are full of stinging fluid.*

## Needle Jab

The hairs on a stinging nettle are hollow tubes made from a glass-like substance called silica. Inside these tiny needles is a stinging liquid that contains formic acid and other damaging chemicals. When an animal brushes against the glassy hairs, their tips break off to expose a sharp point that injects the animal's skin with the potion.

## BRUTAL BIOLOGY

The stinging nettle is not the only plant with a sting. The Australian gympie-gympie stinging tree has a terrible sting—people who have been stung by one describe the sensation as being burned with hot acid while being electrocuted!

## Thorny Tree

The whistling thorn acacia tree has delicious-looking leaves and twigs, but most animals keep far away from this tree for good reason. The plant is covered with big thorns that are up to 3 inches (8 cm) long and are incredibly sharp.

## Prickly Issue

The whistling thorn acacia protects itself with pairs of long, sharp thorns. If an animal gets too close to the spikes, it will be stabbed and cut by them. At the base of each pair of thorns is another nasty surprise. They contain hollow areas that measure about 1 inch (2.5 cm) wide, and are full of stinging ants!

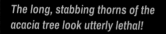

*The long, stabbing thorns of the acacia tree look utterly lethal!*

## Ant Protectors

Different kinds of stinging ants make their nests inside the swollen base of the thorns of the tree, and feed on nectar from the lower part of the acacia's leaves. To protect their homes and food supply, the ants swarm out of their nests to attack any animals that brush against the tree or try to eat parts of it. Luckily for the acacia tree, this ant action protects it too!

# BRUTAL BIOLOGY

When ants leave their nests in search of food, they leave a scent trail. That tells other ants where they are going. Giraffes and some other animals that feed on plants may be able to smell the scent. That could warn them that ants are in the acacia trees, so they know to leave the trees alone.

In the mountains of Chile, South America, is a very unusual plant. It is called the puya, and is found on plains and foothills around the mountains. The plant is armed with daggerlike spikes, which it uses to stab animals that get too close. The lethal stabbers have killed many animals that ventured too near.

## Spiky Protection

Experts believe that the plant's spikes mainly stop animals from reaching the center of the plant, which is where its flowers grow. The puya plant grows huge, colorful flowers that can reach up to 10 feet (3 m) tall. Inside are deep-orange stamens covered in pollen that attracts small birds. They visit the flowers to feed on nectar and by doing so they help pollinate the plant.

*"Puya" is the Mapuche Indian word for "point."*

## Late Bloomers

The puya plant does not have a long time to reproduce, because its flowers grow just once every 15 to 20 years. Once grown, they bloom for only a week. That may be why the plant keeps its flowers protected by a huge wall of spikes.

*The puya flower tower can grow up to 32 feet (10 m) tall!*

# BRUTAL BIOLOGY

The puya's deadly weapons are found at the end of its leaves. When animals become caught on and entangled by the spikes, they cannot escape, and die. Then their bodies decompose, and as they do so, nutrients are released into the ground around the plant. That helps feed the plant so it can grow.

# CHAPTER 5

# HOME INVADERS

Some plants take over an area of land. By doing so, they harm or kill other plants and sometimes animals that live there. But this is just part of the fight for survival—the plants are simply trying to thrive and flourish in their environment.

## What Will Win?

The living things that normally inhabit a particular place are all in competition with each other. They are competing for the things they need to survive, which for plants include water, nutrients, and sunlight. Plants need all these **resources** to make food and keep healthy.

*Algal blooms can cover the surface of water.*

## Space Invaders

Algae are plantlike organisms. They are not plants, but like plants, they make their own food through photosynthesis. Algae live in water, and because there may be a lot of nutrients there, algae can grow and reproduce quickly. When that happens it is called an algal bloom. The downside of this is that the algae take up space and smother other plants. Another problem is that algae live short lives, so as more grow, more die. Then, **bacteria** move into the water, to feed on the dead algae. The bacteria use oxygen to feed, leaving little for fish and other water animals that need the gas in order to breathe.

# BRUTAL BIOLOGY

Some algal blooms can be deadly. That is because each of their cells makes a tiny amount of poison, and when a lot of algae grows, it makes a pool of poison. It can kill animals that drink the water and animals that live in it.

## Strangled to Death

Around the world are famous ruined buildings, covered with incredible tree roots that seem to twist, turn, and wind across the surfaces of the buildings. The trees that twist over them are called strangler figs, or banyans. They may look fascinating, but do not be deceived—they are killers that strangle whatever they crawl across!

## Seed to Strangler

Strangler figs start out as **epiphytes**. These are plants that grow on the branches of other plants, particularly trees. The young seedlings then produce a lot of long roots that grow down a tree trunk and dig into the ground. The young strangler then takes in nutrients and water from the soil. Its roots then grow thicker and merge together, forming a deadly, strangling network around the tree.

*The strangler fig grows wide buttress roots to support it.*

## Killer Tree

As the tree's root network grows, it grips its host tree tighter and tighter. It squeezes the trunk until it cannot take in water, and the host tree begins to die. At the same time, high above, the strangler tree grows branches that are covered with leaves. They block light from the leaves of the host tree, so it cannot make food. Eventually, deprived of food and water, the host tree dies and rots. Just the deadly strangler is left in its place.

# BRUTAL BIOLOGY

Although strangler figs are killers, they are also very important to rain forests. The trees are keystone species, which means they help many other species survive. Fig trees produce fruit several times a year, which forest animals such as monkeys and parrots eat. These animals are in turn foods for **predators**, including jaguars and harpy eagles.

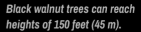

Black walnut trees can reach heights of 150 feet (45 m).

## Monster Poisoner

The black walnut tree of North America is a giant of a tree. It is so big that some plants cannot grow beneath or even near it because the tree blocks out the light and sucks up most of the water nearby through its roots. But those are not the only reasons plants keep away—they do so also because the black walnut is a poisoner!

## A Quick Death

The chemical made by the black walnut that poisons other plants is called juglone. It works by blocking the tubes that transport water through plants, which prevents them from taking in carbon dioxide and oxygen gases. Juglone acts quickly—a plant that comes into contact with the toxin can change from healthy to dead in just two days. The symptoms of walnut poisoning include stunted growth, yellowing leaves, and wilting.

## Poison for Protection

The black walnut produces juglone for protection. The chemical helps stop insects and other animals from eating its parts. It also helps prevent other plants from competing for space and nutrients. The juglone moves through the tree to maximize protection. In spring, a lot of it is found in the young leaves the tree must protect to carry out photosynthesis. In the summer, juglone moves to the roots to keep other plants away and make sure the tree can drink at the driest time of year.

# BRUTAL BIOLOGY

Juglone hangs around even after a black walnut tree has been cut down. In fact, it can take six months for the roots, bark, or woodchips of the cut-down tree to stop being poisonous.

Plants that are easily poisoned by juglone include tomatoes, potatoes, and apple trees.

# CHAPTER 6

# SCARY MENUS

Fruit and vegetables are healthy for us to eat—mainly! However, some parts of plants that we eat contain poison. The poisons are there to keep animals from eating the plants, and we have to be careful not to eat it, too.

## Bitter Rhubarb

The reason that stores sell rhubarb with its leaves cut off is because the leaves, whether they are raw or cooked, contain dangerously high levels of poison. If a person eats too many leaves it can cause serious kidney damage—and even kill them. This rarely happens now because we know about the dangers. Someone would need to eat a huge amount of the bitter leaves to die, but even a small amount can make them sick.

*The cooked stems of the rhubarb plant are delicious and safe to eat, but the leaves can be very dangerous.*

## Beans with Bite

Chili would not taste nearly as good without kidney beans—but never ever try to eat them raw! Raw kidney beans taste bad and are hard to chew, but worse than that, they contain natural toxins called lectins that can cause extreme nausea, vomiting, and an upset stomach. It is vital to soak raw red kidney beans in water for at least five hours and then boil them at high heat until they are soft before eating them.

# BRUTAL BIOLOGY

The mushrooms that we buy in a store are safe and good to eat, but wild mushrooms can be dangerous. Many contain toxins, and the most dangerous of all is the death cap mushroom. Just a few bites of it can kill a person!

*As their name suggests, death cap mushrooms are deadly.*

## Sinister Seeds

People press the seeds of the castor oil plant to extract its oil. The oil can be used for many things, from treating fungal infections to soothing eyes and helping ease joint paint. It is also added to candies, chocolate, and other food. While the plant is very useful, it must be carefully handled—because its seeds are deadly. It only takes one or two seeds to kill a child and up to eight to kill an adult.

*All parts of the castor oil plant are poisonous, which protects it against insect pests such as aphids—but it is the seeds that are the most dangerous.*

_Castor oil seeds that are thousands of years old have even been found in the coffins of the ancient Egyptians, who believed the seeds might be useful in the afterlife._

## Danger Inside

The colorless oil of the castor oil plant has been used by people for centuries, for example, the ancient Egyptians used it for their lamps and as an ointment. Although the plant comes from Africa, it has been planted all over the world. The plant is favoured because it looks good, is very tough, and has clusters of flowers that produce prickly fruits. When the fruits are ripe, they explode and spray the seeds inside them all around to spread the plant to new places. The seeds then have a chance to sink into the soil, where they can sprout and develop—known as **germination** —and grow into new plants.

# BRUTAL BIOLOGY

Castor oil seeds contain a deadly toxin called ricin, which poisons animals such as cattle, horses, sheep, pigs, and rabbits. A poisoned animal will have nausea and vomiting, stomach pains and headaches, diarrhea, fever, and seizures. Eventually, it will die.

The root of the cassava plant contains the **carbohydrate** that people need for energy.

## Deadliest of All?

Cyanide is one of the deadliest poisons in the world. It can cause mild symptoms, such as headaches and dizziness or extreme ones, such as comas and brain disease. A number of plants produce cyanide, including cassava. Despite that, this killer plant is an important source of food for millions of people.

## Filling Food

In parts of Africa, Asia, and South America, people eat cassava roots, known as tubers. They are eaten because they contain large amounts of starch, a type of carbohydrate that is filling and provides people with energy. People eat only the root and not the leaves of the plant, because they release cyanide when eaten.

## Process the Poison

People always process cassava before eating it to stop it releasing cyanide. Some cassava is less dangerous than others, so it can be dried in the sun or boiled to process it. More potent cassava takes longer to make safe. People wash the peeled tubers, grate them, squeeze the grating into a pulp, sieve it, and then soak the remains in water for days before roasting. Even then, they must be cooked before they are safe to eat.

# BRUTAL BIOLOGY

When animals and people chew cassava, it breaks down the plant cell walls and releases a chemical—linamarase. That chemical can change other chemicals into cyanide. Scientists are trying to treat cancer by using linamarase to produce cyanide that zaps only cancer **cells**, and not healthy ones.

*Rats have burrowed beneath this cassava plant. Rats and mice try to feed on the plant, so it makes poison to try and deter them.*

# SUPER SURVIVORS

Deadly plants use a wide variety of weapons for protection or to survive in their environment. They include thorns, toxins, and other extreme tactics to harm fellow living things. The plants use their weapons to stop other organisms from damaging and eating them, or preventing them from reproducing. Many plants also have ways to warn animals that they are dangerous even before animals bite or touch them.

*Rosary peas are red for a reason—they are poisonous!*

## Warning with Red

Some plants show they are dangerous by growing long, sharp thorns that can be clearly seen. Others display warning colors, for example, rosary peas are a bright red color, which is often used in nature as a danger sign. These peas contain abrin, which is a deadly poison. They were named for their use in strings of rosary beads and have also been used in jewelry, before people were aware how toxic the peas are.

## Smelly and Strange

Other plants use bad tastes and smells, or strange milky-looking **sap**, to stop them being eaten. Euphorbia plants have a highly toxic, milky sap. The sap helps seal wounds if the plant stem is broken, and it has antibacterial properties that stop the plant becoming infected with diseases. The sap looks nasty, which warns animals that it will give them a burning sensation if they harm the plant. Like all living things, plants have adapted to help them better survive in the world around them. Their weapons and poisons are tools for ensuring they continue to live. As long as animals, including people, heed the warnings plants give, they can survive alongside them.

## BRUTAL BIOLOGY

Not all dangerous plants come with a warning label! For example, the oleander is a beautiful plant with colorful flowers and soft leaves, but it is highly toxic if eaten and can irritate the skin when handled.

*The euphorbia plant looks pretty, but it has a very toxic sap.*

# GLOSSARY

**bacteria** single-celled living things, some of which can be harmful

**carbohydrate** a food type that is a source of energy for our bodies

**carnivorous** describes a plant or animal that feeds on animals

**cells** the microscopically small building blocks of living things

**digested** broken down inside the body to get nutrients

**enzymes** substances that help chemical reactions happen inside the bodies of living things

**epiphytes** plants that grow high up on other plants or trees to reach light

**fruit** the part of a plant that contains and protects its seeds

**germination** the process where a seed starts to sprout and develop

**glands** organs in the body with a particular job to do, such as make sweat or release substances called hormones that tell the body how to work and how to grow

**hosts** animals or plants on which parasites live

**immune** resistant to or protected against a disease or danger

**insects** small animals that have six legs and generally one or two pairs of wings

**nectar** the sugary substance found in plants

**nutrients** the chemicals that nourish living things and help them live and grow

**organisms** living things

**paralyzes** causes something to be wholly or partly incapable of movement

**photosynthesis** the process by which a plant makes its own food

**pollen** a powder made by the male part of a flower

**pollinate** a process in which pollen travels from one flower to another and causes seeds to grow there

**predators** animals that catch and eat other animals

**prey** an animal that is caught and eaten by other animals

**reproduce** to have offspring

**resources** things that can be used or have value, such as oil

**roots** plant parts that grow underground

**sap** a sugary liquid containing food made in a plant's leaves

**species** a type of living thing

**stamens** the parts of flowers that produce pollen

**stem** the part of the plant that holds it upright and supports its flowers and leaves

**toxins** poisons

**tropical** describes a region that is very hot because it is close to the equator

# FIND OUT MORE

## Books

Honda, Kathleen J. and Makoto Honda. *Venus Flytrap—A Science Guide for Kids & Teachers*. Independently Published, 2022.

Markovics, Joyce. *Carnivorous Plants* (Beware! Killer Plants). Cherry Lake Publishing, 2021.

Thorogood, Chris. *When Plants Took Over the Planet: The Amazing Story of Plant Evolution* (Incredible Evolution). QED Publishing, 2021.

## Websites

Find out more about killer plants at:
**https://kids.britannica.com/students/article/poisonous-plants/276455**

Learn more about flesh-eating plants at:
**https://kids.kiddle.co/Carnivorous_plant**

There are lots of fun facts about plants at:
**www.sciencekids.co.nz/sciencefacts/plants.html**

**Publisher's note to educators and parents:**
All the websites featured above have been carefully reviewed to ensure that they are suitable for students. However, many websites change often, and we cannot guarantee that a site's future contents will continue to meet our high standards of educational value. Please be advised that students should be closely monitored whenever they access the Internet.

# INDEX

## About the Authors

Kelly Roberts is an experienced children's book author who has always been fascinated by the natural world. She has written many science and nature books for children. Louise Spilsbury has written hundreds of children's information books about our natural world.